HOW TO HAVE A LUCID DREAM:

A Practical Guide to Awakening Within Your Dreams

Marc Reynolds

Crafty Fox Publishing

"To dream lucidly is not to escape reality—it is to witness the mind at its most honest, creative, and free."

—MARC REYNOLDS

CONTENTS

Title Page
Epigraph
Preface
Chapter 1: Introduction to Lucid Dreaming — 1
Chapter 2: Preparing for Lucid Dreaming — 5
Chapter 3: Dream Recall Techniques — 9
Chapter 4: Lucid Dream Induction Methods — 14
Chapter 5: Navigating the Lucid Dream World — 22
Chapter 6: Common Symbols and Dream Themes — 29
Chapter 7: Deepening Your Lucid Dream Practice — 37
Chapter 8: Troubleshooting & FAQs — 44
Chapter 9: Integrating Lucid Dreams Into Daily Life — 49
Chapter 10: Final Reflections & Next Steps — 56
About The Author — 67
Books By This Author — 69

PREFACE

Creativity, like any skill—or any muscle—needs exercise. It doesn't flourish by chance or talent alone. It grows stronger through use, through attention, and through deliberate cultivation.

Lucidity is often mistaken as a way to escape—an invitation to disappear into a subconscious playground, a virtual fantasy world where anything is possible. But that's not what this book is about. Lucid dreaming isn't about running away. It's about learning to tune into the most powerful, untapped tool you already have: your creative subconscious.

We've all had those moments. You sit with a problem or dilemma for hours, going in mental circles. No clarity. No breakthrough. But then—you give up. You walk away, take a break, maybe even take a nap. And suddenly… the answer appears. Clear. Effortless. Obvious. That's your subconscious speaking. That's the creative spark working behind the scenes.

What if you could access that spark more intentionally?

Lucid dreaming is a gateway to that space. A space where insight surfaces, not by force, but by allowing your mind to loosen, to wander, to connect in unexpected ways. The same mechanism that solves problems while you sleep can be trained, strengthened, and consciously explored.

I believe creativity and imagination, drawn from the deepest layers of our subconscious, are what truly make us human. They are not luxuries—they are our greatest assets.

This book is a guide to waking up within your dreams—not just to explore fantastic worlds, but to strengthen the very core of your creative mind.

Exercise it. Trust it. And let it show you what's possible.

— Marc Reynolds

CHAPTER 1: INTRODUCTION TO LUCID DREAMING

What is Lucid Dreaming?

Lucid dreaming occurs when you're aware that you're dreaming while still within the dream itself. Unlike regular dreams, where events unfold without conscious influence, lucid dreams offer you the opportunity to consciously navigate, control, and interact with your dream environment. This state provides a unique and powerful bridge between your conscious mind and subconscious world.

Many people enjoy lucid dreams for their potential to experience fantastical adventures and scenarios otherwise impossible in waking life, such as flying freely, exploring alien landscapes, or even having superhuman abilities like telekinesis or incredible strength. These vivid experiences not only provide entertainment but can also offer profound emotional and psychological insights.

However, there are common misconceptions surrounding lucid dreaming. Some people mistakenly believe lucid dreaming means absolute control over every aspect of the dream or that it requires a special talent accessible only to a few. In reality, while lucid dreams can offer significant influence over dream scenarios, complete and total control is rare. Instead, lucidity more commonly provides heightened awareness and varying degrees of interaction and influence within the dream environment.

Another misconception is that lucid dreaming might disrupt sleep or lead to exhaustion. Scientific evidence suggests that when practiced responsibly, lucid dreaming occurs naturally within normal sleep cycles and doesn't negatively impact overall sleep quality. This book will provide scientifically supported methods to help you achieve lucidity effectively and safely, enriching both your dream experiences and your waking life.

Historical Background and Pioneers

The concept of lucid dreaming is not new. Ancient Greek philosopher Aristotle (384–322 BC) first described dream-awareness in his work "On Dreams," noting instances where dreamers recognize they're dreaming. Modern lucid dreaming began with pioneers such as the French scholar Marquis d'Hervey de Saint-Denys, who documented his experiences and methods for inducing lucidity in the 19th century. In 1913, psychiatrist Frederik van Eeden formally introduced the term "lucid dream," describing the dreamer's clear awareness and ability to direct the dream consciously.

In the late 20th century, researchers like Celia Green and Keith Hearne provided scientific evidence of lucid dreaming, with Hearne conducting the first lab experiments verifying lucid dreaming through eye-movement signals in 1975.

However, it was American psychophysiologist Stephen LaBerge, founder of the Lucidity Institute, who popularized lucid dreaming scientifically. LaBerge developed induction methods such as the Mnemonic Induction of Lucid Dreams (MILD) and authored widely read books like *Exploring the World of Lucid Dreaming*.

The Science Behind Lucid Dreaming

Lucid dreaming predominantly occurs during Rapid Eye Movement (REM) sleep, the sleep stage where most vivid dreams happen. During lucid dreams, scientific studies have revealed distinct neurological patterns. Researchers such as Ursula Voss discovered that lucid dreaming is characterized by increased brain activity in the gamma frequency (~40 Hz) within the frontal cortex, an area associated with self-awareness and conscious thought.

Furthermore, brain imaging studies led by cognitive neuroscientist Martin Dresler demonstrated that lucid dreaming involves increased activation in regions like the dorsolateral prefrontal cortex, responsible for executive functioning and reality-checking—areas normally less active during regular dreams.

These neurological insights indicate that lucid dreaming is a unique "hybrid" state, mixing wakefulness and sleep in ways measurable through modern neuroscience.

Benefits of Lucid Dreaming

Lucid dreaming isn't just fascinating—it offers practical benefits for emotional well-being, creativity, and personal growth:

- **Creativity Enhancement:** Lucid dreams provide a limitless playground for exploring creative ideas, from art and literature to innovative problem-solving, as evidenced by numerous artists, writers, and scientists who've used lucid dreams for inspiration.
- **Overcoming Nightmares:** Clinically recognized in therapeutic settings, lucid dreaming helps individuals gain control over recurring nightmares, reducing anxiety and fear associated with conditions such as PTSD.
- **Personal Insight and Self-Discovery:** Through lucid dreaming, individuals can interact directly with their subconscious minds, uncovering deeper personal truths, confronting fears safely, and fostering personal growth.

This book will guide you through scientifically-backed methods and practical techniques to achieve lucidity reliably, equipping you with skills that can enrich both your dream experiences and waking life.

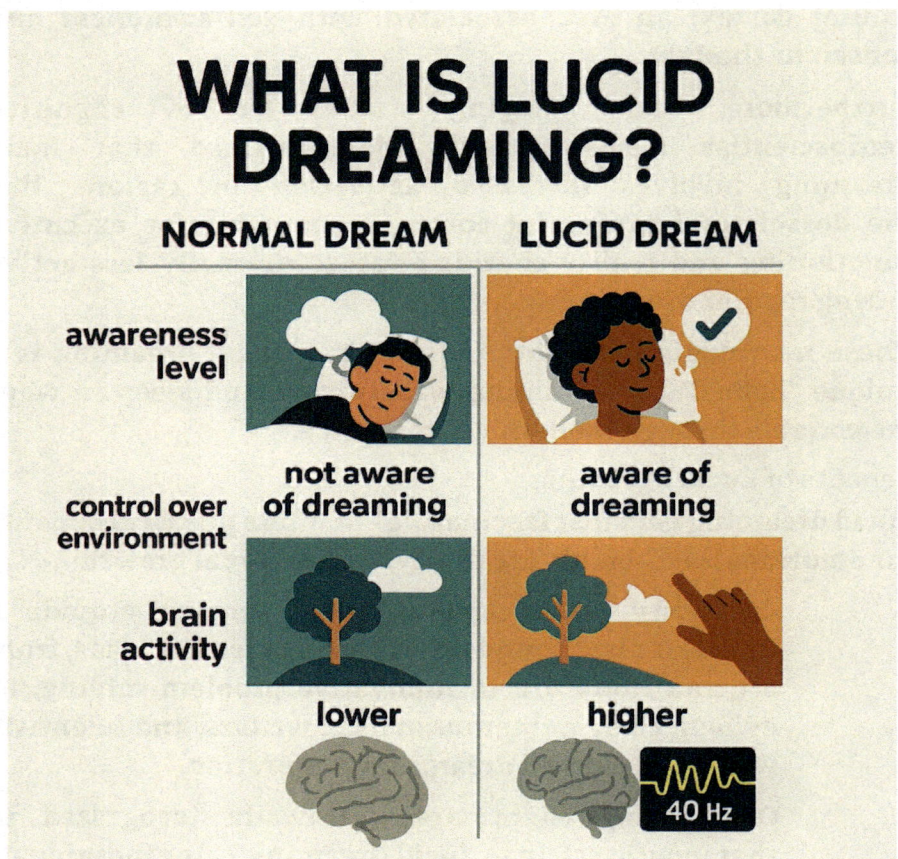

CHAPTER 2: PREPARING FOR LUCID DREAMING

Setting an Intention: The Power of Mindset and Belief

One of the foundational aspects of successful lucid dreaming is setting a clear and powerful intention. Scientific studies, including those by Stephen LaBerge and Ursula Voss, have highlighted how intention-setting activates brain regions associated with self-awareness and prospective memory—remembering to perform intended actions in the future.

Before sleep, clearly affirm to yourself, "Tonight, I will realize I'm dreaming." Reinforce this intention by vividly visualizing yourself becoming lucid within a dream scenario. Imagine how it will feel when you recognize you are dreaming. Picture specific cues or events in the dream that will trigger your lucidity. The stronger, clearer, and more emotionally charged your intention, the more effectively it will carry over into your dreams.

Setting a strong intention also significantly enhances dream recall. By programming your subconscious mind to remember your dreams vividly upon waking, you reinforce neural pathways associated with memory and awareness. Studies indicate that individuals who regularly set clear intentions experience improved dream recall, enabling them to capture more detail and recognize recurring themes or symbols within their dreams.

Recent studies by Ursula Voss have further shown that external brain stimulation, specifically at 40 Hz gamma frequency, can significantly increase the likelihood of inducing lucid dreams. This stimulation appears to activate neural networks associated with self-awareness, demonstrating that targeted brain activity plays a direct role in achieving lucidity.

Ultimately, a focused and intentional mindset not only primes your subconscious for lucidity but also ensures a stronger connection to your dreams, laying the groundwork for a robust lucid dreaming practice.

Creating a Dream-Friendly Sleep Environment

The environment you create before and during sleep plays a crucial role in determining the quality of your dreams and your ability to become lucid. A well-optimized sleep setting not only supports better rest but also enhances REM sleep, which is where most vivid and lucid dreams occur.

Here are several elements to consider when designing your dream-friendly sleep environment:

- **Lighting:** A dark room helps trigger melatonin production, essential for restful sleep and healthy REM cycles. Use blackout curtains or an eye mask to eliminate outside light. Consider soft, dim lighting in the hour before bed to signal your body that it's time to wind down.
- **Sound:** Reduce environmental noise that can disrupt sleep cycles. If you live in a noisy area, white noise machines, calming nature sounds, or earplugs can help create a consistent auditory backdrop that supports deep sleep.
- **Temperature:** Keep your bedroom cool, ideally around 16–19°C (60–67°F). Overheating or being too cold can interrupt your sleep cycles and reduce the likelihood of long, uninterrupted REM periods.

- **Clutter-Free Space:** A tidy and uncluttered room can reduce mental distractions. A clean environment promotes a sense of calm and focus, which can carry into your mental state as you fall asleep.
- **Scent:** Scents like lavender or chamomile, used through essential oils or pillow sprays, can encourage relaxation. Some studies show they promote better sleep quality and increase the chances of dream vividness.
- **Dream Tools:** Keep your dream journal and a pen by your bed so you can record dreams immediately upon waking. This not only improves recall but also builds a subconscious expectation that dreams are important and worth remembering.

Creating a sleep environment that promotes relaxation, comfort, and mental clarity supports all other lucid dreaming practices. When your physical space is aligned with your intentions, your mind is more likely to transition into rich, vivid dreams—and potentially, into lucid ones.

Sleep Hygiene and Why it Matters

Good sleep hygiene is essential for lucid dreaming. It supports the depth and consistency of your REM cycles—the fertile ground for dream awareness. Keeping a regular sleep schedule ensures your body naturally progresses into longer and more vivid REM periods, especially toward the early morning hours.

Research has consistently shown that individuals who prioritize high-quality sleep are more likely to experience lucid dreams. This includes reducing exposure to artificial light before bed, avoiding screens, and winding down with calming activities.

Substances like caffeine and alcohol can significantly impact your ability to achieve lucidity. Caffeine, a known stimulant, can delay sleep onset and reduce the time spent in REM sleep. Alcohol, while it may help you fall asleep faster, tends to fragment sleep and suppress REM early in the night—followed by a rebound effect later, which may lead to intense and chaotic dreaming rather than lucidity.

However, some compounds have been explored for their potential to enhance lucid dreaming. Supplements like galantamine, when taken responsibly and in moderation, have shown promise in increasing lucidity. That said, these should be used cautiously and only after establishing a strong foundation in natural induction techniques. The risks, side effects, and individual variability in response make it important that supplements are approached as a secondary aid—not a shortcut.

Overall, practicing consistent, mindful sleep hygiene is the most sustainable and healthy way to prepare your body and mind for lucid dreaming. It not only enhances your chances of having a lucid dream but also improves the quality of your overall rest and well-being.

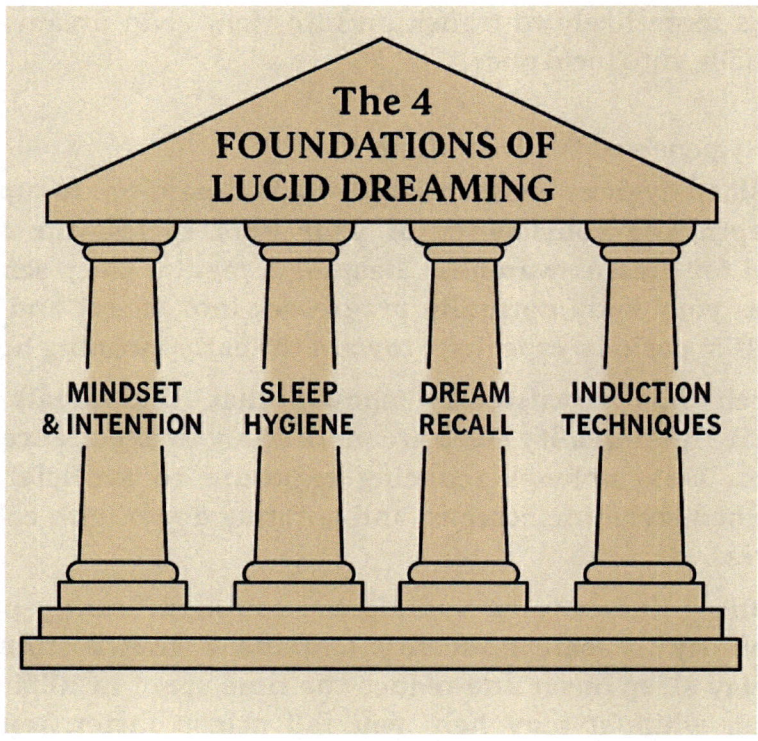

CHAPTER 3: DREAM RECALL TECHNIQUES

The Importance of Remembering Dreams

Before you can become lucid in your dreams, you need to remember them. Dream recall is the foundation of lucid dreaming. Without it, you may have lucid dreams and never know it. The more vividly and consistently you remember your dreams, the more familiar you become with your personal dream patterns—and the more likely you are to recognize when you're dreaming.

Dream recall also strengthens the feedback loop between your waking and dreaming mind. Every time you recall and record a dream, you're telling your brain that dreams are meaningful. This reinforces the cognitive processes that support dream awareness, meta-cognition, and ultimately, lucidity.

How to Improve Dream Recall

1. Keeping a Dream Journal

The most effective way to improve dream recall is to keep a dedicated dream journal. Place it within reach of your bed, and write down everything you remember immediately upon waking—even if it's only fragments, emotions, or colors.

Speed is key. Dream memories fade rapidly after waking, sometimes within seconds. That's why it's crucial to capture whatever you can recall *right away*—before moving, speaking, or looking at a screen. A good dream journal should make this process effortless.

Using a prompt journal—a journal that provides structured questions or cues—is ideal. You don't need to figure out what to write or how to organize your entry. Simply read the prompt, answer it, and move on. This reduces mental friction and keeps your focus on the memory itself rather than the format.

While technology offers convenience, pen and paper remains the most accessible and reliable method—especially in the groggy moments right after waking. Writing by hand avoids the distractions of smartphones and tablets, which can easily pull you into notifications or blue light exposure. A notebook requires no boot-up time and can be used comfortably even when you're half asleep.

Tips for journaling:

- Use headings like Date, Dream Title, Description, Emotions, Symbols, and Reflections.
- Write in the present tense to make it feel more immediate.
- Include any recurring elements or unusual experiences.

With time, this practice significantly increases the richness and detail of your dream memory.

Looking for a ready-to-use dream journal? I've created two guided journals designed to help you record dreams quickly and effectively—even when you're half asleep. Each journal includes structured prompts to reduce friction, capture essential details, and build the habit of recall:

- *Dream Journal: Dream Relax Reflect Remember Embrace* – Available on Amazon
- *Dream Journal: Dream relax reflect remember embrace* – Available on Amazon

These journals are pen-and-paper friendly—perfect for nightstands—and won't distract you like a glowing phone screen might. They're made to be used the moment you wake up.

Dream Details

Date: _____

Dream Title: _____

Description: (Write a summary of the dream in as much detail as possible.)

_____
_____
_____
_____
_____
_____

Emotions Felt During the Dream:

☐ Happy ☐ Sad ☐ Fearful ☐ Confused ☐ Excited ☐ Angry ☐ Peaceful

☐ Other: _____

People or Figures in the Dream:

(List key characters or people in the dream.)

_____
_____

Symbols & Objects:

(What stood out? E.g., animals, numbers, objects, colors, places.)

_____
_____

Dream Reflection

Actions & Events:
(What happened? List or describe key moments in order.)

Possible Meanings or Associations: (Does this dream relate to anything in your life? Does it remind you of something?)

How the Dream Made You Feel Upon Waking:
☐ Calm ☐ Confused ☐ Anxious ☐ Inspired ☐ Other:

Lucid or Not? ☐ Yes ☐ No

When and How Did You Recall This Dream?

Notes & Additional Thoughts:

Sketch Box: scene, symbol, or feeling from the dream

---

2. Using Affirmations Before Bed

Just as intention-setting helps induce lucid dreams, it also primes your brain for remembering them. Repeat to yourself as you fall asleep:

"I will remember my dreams when I wake up."

This affirmation programs your subconscious mind to retain

dream content and strengthens your commitment to dream recall.

3. Waking Up Gently

How you wake up can influence how much you remember. Jarring alarms can disrupt dream recall. Instead:

- Use a gentle alarm sound or natural light alarm clock.
- When you first wake up, lie still with your eyes closed.
- Mentally retrace your steps: "Where was I just now? What was I feeling?"

This moment—right after waking—is when your dream memories are most fragile and easiest to catch.

4. Tagging Dream Signs

Dream signs are recurring themes, characters, places, or oddities unique to your dream world. When reviewing your dream journal, highlight or underline these elements.

By recognizing your personal dream signs, you'll start noticing patterns that can serve as triggers for lucidity in future dreams.

Summary

Improving dream recall is not just about memory—it's about creating a habit of attention and awareness that carries over into your dreams. With consistent practice, you'll begin to remember more dreams with greater clarity, setting the stage for reliable and repeatable lucid dreaming experiences.

Even if you don't recall a dream one night, don't skip the journaling habit. Write "no recall" to maintain the practice and keep the habit alive. Over time, your brain will get the message: dreams matter.

CHAPTER 4: LUCID DREAM INDUCTION METHODS

Lucid dreaming may feel spontaneous for some, but it's very much a skill you can learn. By combining the foundational practices you've built so far—intention-setting, healthy sleep habits, and consistent dream recall—you're ready to use proven induction methods. These techniques strengthen your awareness within the dream state, enabling you to realize that you're dreaming while it's happening.

In this chapter, we'll explore several widely recognized methods: *Reality Checks, Mnemonic Induction (MILD), Wake Back to Bed (WBTB),* and *Wake-Initiated Lucid Dreaming (WILD)*. We'll also address supplements and herbs that some enthusiasts use to enhance lucidity.

---

1. Reality Checks (Reality Testing)

What are Reality Checks?
Reality checks are simple tests you perform during waking life to confirm whether you're dreaming or not. By building the habit of testing your reality daily, you'll eventually perform it within a dream—and notice that the "test" yields an impossible or bizarre result, triggering lucidity.

How to Do It:

Choose a Simple Test: Examples include:

- **Hand Check:** Count your fingers or examine your palm. In dreams, fingers may appear distorted or change count.
- **Text Test:** Look at text, look away, then look back. In dreams, text often morphs or dissolves on second glance.
- **Nose Pinch:** Pinch your nose and try to breathe. In a dream, you'll still be able to breathe.

2. **Ingrain the Habit:** Perform your chosen test multiple times a day—at least 5–10. Do it mindfully, really questioning, "Am I awake or dreaming?"
3. **Link to Dream Signs:** If you identified recurring dream signs from Chapter 3, do a reality check whenever you see something similar in waking life.

Why It Works:

Dreams commonly replicate everyday scenarios, but with glitches. By making reality-checking a reflex, you transfer that habit into dreams—where you'll notice the glitch and realize you're in a dream.

Cognitive Underpinnings of Reality Testing

Research on habit-formation and metacognition provides insight into why reality checks carry over into dreams. Psychologists studying prospective memory—the ability to remember intended actions in the future—have shown that tasks repeated consciously during the day can re-emerge in dream states. By performing reality checks regularly, you're training your brain to stay alert for anomalies in any context, including when you're asleep.

In a 2017 large-scale study on lucid dreaming techniques led by Denholm Aspy, participants who consistently practiced reality checks (often combined with additional methods) reported higher rates of dream awareness. This supports the idea that daily, deliberate habit-building primes the mind to detect the dream world's oddities.

Success Stories and Community Evidence

Workshops hosted by the Lucidity Institute, as well as numerous online lucid dreaming forums, are brimming with accounts of how reality checks triggered someone's first lucid moment. A common scenario is the nose-pinch test: after several days of practice in waking life, a person finds themselves pinching their nose in a dream—and realizing they can still breathe. This instant contradiction sparks the excited realization, "I must be dreaming!"

Thus, reality checks bridge cognitive psychology (habit-building and prospective memory) with dream science (consciousness in REM). Repetition makes the act so routine that it naturally appears in dreams, revealing the dream state the moment a check behaves in an impossible way.

2. Mnemonic Induction of Lucid Dreams (MILD)

Origin: Popularized by Dr. Stephen LaBerge, MILD is a cornerstone of lucid dream training. It leverages the power of intention and prospective memory—the ability to remember to do something in the future.

Core Steps:

1. **Recall a Recent Dream:** Upon waking (especially during the night or early morning), lie still and focus on the dream you just had.

2. **Identify a Dream Cue:** Pinpoint a moment in the dream that could have alerted you to dreaming (something strange or illogical).

3. **Visualize Becoming Lucid:** Replay that dream scene in your mind, but this time, imagine noticing the cue and *realizing* you're in a dream. Feel the excitement and clarity of the moment.

4. **Affirm Your Intention:** As you fall back asleep, mentally repeat a phrase such as, "Next time I'm

dreaming, I *will* recognize that I'm dreaming."

Tips & Best Practices:

- **Combine with Dream Recall:** The more details you remember from your dreams, the easier it is to identify potential cues.
- **Time It Right:** MILD is especially effective after 4–6 hours of sleep, when your REM periods grow longer.
- **Stay Focused:** Try not to let your mind wander; keep replaying and affirming until you drift off.

Studies by researchers like Denholm Aspy have shown that MILD significantly increases lucidity rates when applied consistently and combined with strong dream recall.

3. Wake Back to Bed (WBTB)

Why It Works:

Humans experience more frequent and prolonged REM sleep in the later half of the night. By briefly waking yourself after several hours, you return to sleep during a high-intensity REM window. With your mind slightly more alert, it's easier to recognize when a dream begins.

How to Do It:

1. **Sleep for 4–6 Hours:** Set an alarm or naturally wake up during the early morning.
2. **Stay Awake Briefly:** Get out of bed for 10–30 minutes. Read about lucid dreaming or jot notes in your dream journal to keep your mind engaged but not overstimulated.
3. **Return to Bed:** With fresh focus, lie down and use MILD or a mindfulness approach. Keep reminding yourself, "I will become lucid."
4. **Enter REM Quickly:** Because of your circadian timing, you're more likely to drop into REM soon, carrying that alert mindset into your dream.

Best Practices:

- Experiment with the length of wake time—too short and you might remain groggy; too long and you risk full wakefulness.
- Maintain a relaxed but focused mental state. If you become too awake (e.g., scrolling your phone), it might be hard to fall asleep.
- Pair WBTB with MILD or reality checks for maximum effect.

Research frequently shows that WBTB combined with MILD can dramatically boost success rates, sometimes leading to lucidity in as little as one week of practice.

4. Wake-Initiated Lucid Dream (WILD)

What Is WILD?

WILD is a method where you maintain consciousness from wakefulness directly into the dream state, witnessing the dream form around you. This can result in highly vivid and stable lucid dreams, but it's considered more advanced.

Steps to Attempt WILD:

Relax Body Completely: Lie comfortably on your back or side. Gradually release tension in each muscle group.

1. Focus the Mind: Use a mental anchor—such as counting, focusing on the breath, or visualizing a simple scene—to stay aware as your body falls asleep.
2. Observe Hypnagogic Imagery: You may see flashes of light, shapes, or hear sounds. Keep calm and let them flow. Resist the urge to move or startle yourself awake.
3. Transition to a Dream: Eventually, these images coalesce into a full dream scene or you feel a shift. Perform a gentle reality check to confirm you've crossed the threshold.

Tips:

- **Best During WBTB:** Attempt WILD after 4–5 hours of sleep. Falling into REM more quickly makes the process smoother.
- **Expect Weird Sensations:** Vibrations, buzzing noises, or a sense of floating are common. Understand they're harmless byproducts of the mind-sleep transition.
- **Stay Calm:** Getting excited can jolt you awake.

WILD takes practice; many beginners find it challenging. However, success can yield some of the most exhilarating lucid dreams because you begin lucid right from the start.

5. Supplements and Herbs

Caution First:
While some substances are believed to facilitate REM intensity or dream vividness, always approach them with caution. Research is ongoing, and responses vary widely.

Commonly Discussed Options:

1. **Galantamine:** A mild cognitive enhancer derived from certain flowers, often cited in lucid dreaming circles. Studies suggest it can boost acetylcholine levels, which may promote REM activity. Must be taken carefully—preferably with medical guidance.
2. **Choline Bitartrate:** Another supplement that supports acetylcholine production, sometimes combined with galantamine.
3. **Mugwort:** A herb traditionally linked to enhanced dreaming. Anecdotal reports claim more vivid dreams, though scientific evidence is limited.
4. **Vitamin B6:** Some dreamers claim it intensifies dreams.

Pros & Cons:

- **Pros:** Potentially increases dream vividness and awareness, especially if you already practice induction

methods.
- **Cons:** Some substances disrupt normal sleep architecture or cause side effects (headaches, nausea, etc.). Over-reliance may hinder natural skill-building.

Always consult a healthcare professional before experimenting, and treat supplements as an *optional addition* rather than a main strategy.

Pulling It All Together

1. **Start With Strong Foundations:** Chapter 1 and 2's guidance on mindset and environment are crucial. Combining consistent dream recall (Chapter 3) with these induction methods amplifies results.
2. **Experiment and Adapt:** Each method can be customized to fit your lifestyle. Mix and match (e.g., MILD + WBTB or Reality Checks + WBTB) to see what yields the best results.
3. **Stay Consistent and Patient:** Lucid dreaming is a learnable skill, but it rarely happens overnight. Keep a positive attitude, track your progress in a journal, and refine your technique over time.

By practicing these induction methods diligently, you'll train your mind to become aware *during* the dream state. Whether you're a beginner or honing advanced skills, reality checks, MILD, WBTB, and WILD form the core toolkit for stepping into a lucid dream—where your only limit is imagination.

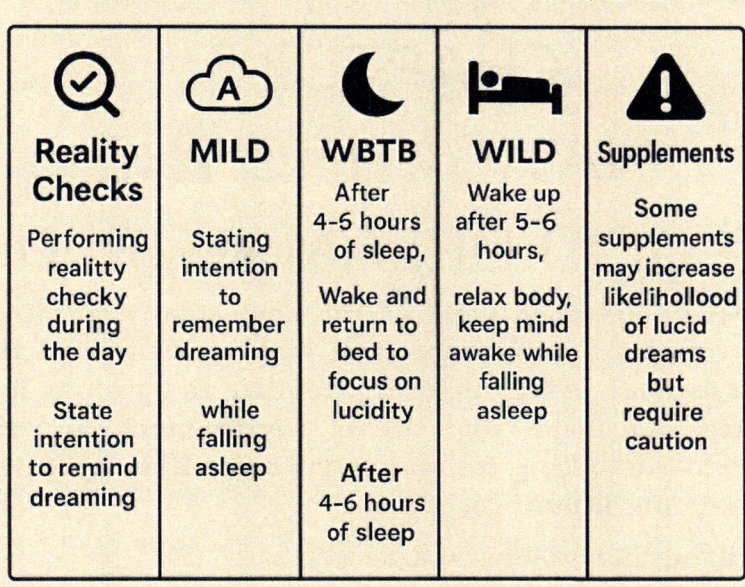

CHAPTER 5: NAVIGATING THE LUCID DREAM WORLD

Once you've achieved lucidity, the next step is learning how to stay in that dream state—and make the most of it. This chapter focuses on techniques to stabilize and prolong lucidity, influence and shape your dream environment, and explore safely while handling common challenges like nightmares or overwhelming situations.

1. Stabilizing and Prolonging Lucidity

Many first-time lucid dreamers find the excitement of realizing "I'm dreaming!" can quickly yank them out of sleep. The surge of adrenaline often leads to premature awakening or losing lucidity as the dream destabilizes. Below are proven ways to maintain that balance between awareness and relaxation.

Grounding Techniques

Two techniques studied extensively by pioneering lucid dreaming researcher **Stephen LaBerge** have consistently shown to increase dream stability, duration, and clarity:

    1. Rubbing Your Hands Together:
- Quickly rub your dream-hands together, feeling their friction, texture, and warmth. This grounding sensation engages your senses within the dream, anchoring your awareness and preventing you from

accidentally waking up. LaBerge's research found this simple act markedly improved dream clarity and prolonged the lucid experience.

2. **Spinning in Place:**
   - When you feel lucidity fading, gently spin your dream body around. As you spin, remind yourself, "This is my dream." According to LaBerge's influential studies at the Lucidity Institute, spinning significantly reduces premature awakenings and increases dream vividness, helping you stay lucid longer..

3. **Verbal Commands:**
   - Say out loud (in the dream) phrases like "Clarity now!" or "Increase lucidity!" Many dreamers report the environment grows sharper when they confidently issue these commands.

4. **Focusing on an Object:**
   - Engage your senses, focus on nearby detail: the texture of a wall or your dream-hands. Observing the fine points helps anchor you to the dream scene and prolong lucidity.

These methods work by engaging your senses within the dream so your mind won't default to waking up. Think of it like grabbing hold of the dream before it slips away.

1.2 Calming Emotions

Excitement is normal—especially for your first few lucid dreams—but too much can jar you awake. Try taking a deep breath and reminding yourself you have plenty of time. Approach a lucid dream with curiosity, not urgency.

- **Slow Breathing:** Inhale through your nose, exhale through your mouth, concentrating on each breath.

- **Mindful Observation:** Tell yourself, "I have time. Let me explore slowly," and then look around to take in small details of the dreamscape.

Practice these calm responses in your waking day so they become second nature in a dream.

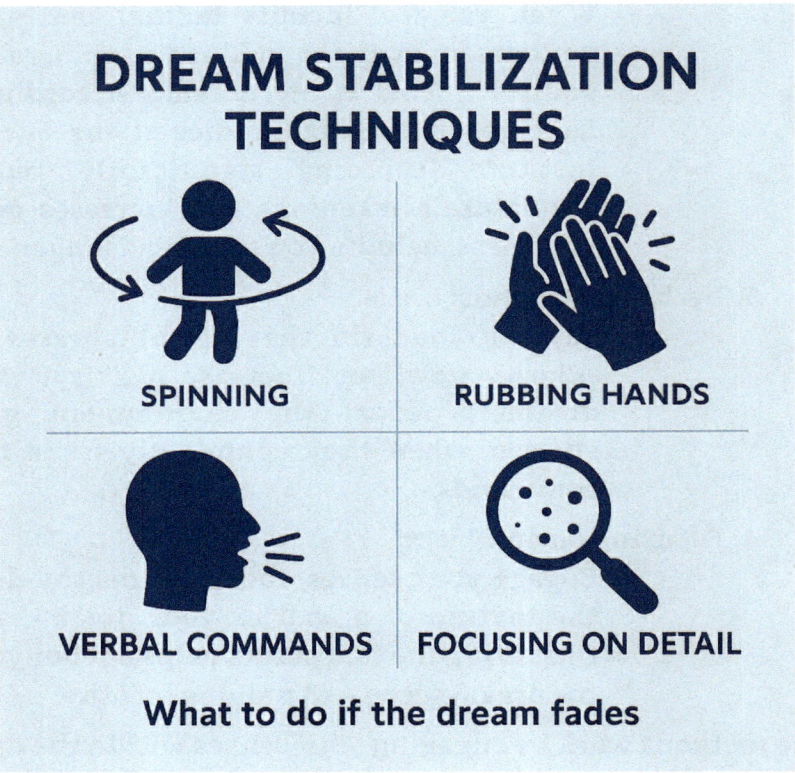

2. Shaping and Influencing Your Dream

One of the great joys of lucid dreaming is the ability to intentionally alter your dream environment—akin to having a personal sandbox or virtual reality that responds to your thoughts.

2.1 Changing the Scene

- **Door Method:** Picture a door and believe that on the other side is your desired location. Open it, and walk into a new scene.

- **Spontaneous Visualization:** Close your dream-eyes (briefly!) and imagine a beach, a spaceship, or any setting you desire. Reopen them and see the environment morph accordingly.

2.2 Altering Dream Elements

- **Object Summoning:** Want a tool, a musical instrument, or a companion? Look away or behind you while expecting the item to be there when you turn around.
- **Flying:** A hallmark of lucid dreams. If you have trouble taking off, use a small jump or imagine a gust of wind lifting you. Some people flap their arms or use a mental "boost" by shouting a command, e.g., "Up!"

2.3 Interacting with Dream Figures

Dream characters can be friendly, neutral, or occasionally adversarial. You can:

- **Ask Questions:** Some lucid dreamers seek advice from characters who represent facets of their subconscious.
- **Collaborate or Confront:** If a figure is hostile or cryptic, try calmly talking to them. Research has shown that fear-based dream interactions can become healing moments when faced directly.

3. Safe Exploration and Dealing with Challenges

Lucid dreams are generally safe and positive experiences, but sometimes unsettling or frightening scenarios may occur. Rather than immediately waking yourself up, lucid dreaming provides a uniquely effective opportunity to face these challenges constructively.

3.1 Overcoming Nightmares

Research from the Lucidity Institute emphasizes the remarkable effectiveness of confronting nightmares directly within lucid dreams. In their studies, lucid dreamers who intentionally engaged nightmare figures reported significantly fewer recurring nightmares and reduced anxiety overall. This aligns closely with clinical studies, notably by Spoormaker and van den Bout (2006), demonstrating that lucid dreaming acts as a therapeutic tool for those experiencing chronic nightmares or anxiety-related sleep disturbances.

Practical ways to confront nightmares include:

- **Dialogue and Interaction:**
  Calmly approach threatening figures and ask directly, "Why are you here?" or "What do you represent?" This act of confrontation often reduces fear and provides meaningful insight.

- **Transforming the Dream Scenario:**
  Use your lucid awareness to alter the narrative actively. You can shrink or transform frightening dream elements into harmless or friendly forms, reinforcing your control.

Empowering Verbal Commands:
Clearly state commands within your dream like, "I am in control. You cannot harm me." This confident approach reinforces your conscious power and effectively dissipates fear.

3.2 Handling Overly Vivid Scenes

Some lucid dreamers experience scenarios so vivid they become disorienting. If the content is intense (e.g., realistic conflicts or emotional overload):

1. **Stabilize First:** Use grounding techniques (spinning, hand-rubbing).

2. **Change the Mood:** Command the dream to become calmer: "Let this dream be peaceful."

3. **Exit If Needed:** Sometimes it's best to wake up gently. You can do this by focusing on your real body, blinking rapidly in the dream, or simply deciding to open your "real" eyes.

3.3 Avoiding 'False Awakenings'

A false awakening is when you "wake up" in your bedroom—only to discover it's still a dream. This can loop multiple times, causing confusion. To handle this:

- **Perform a Reality Check Whenever You 'Wake Up':** This habit ensures you recognize false awakenings quickly.
- **Keep Calm:** If you discover you're still dreaming, use it as another chance for exploration or simply try to wake for real by focusing on your physical body's position in bed.

4. Example Scenarios for Practice

Flying Over a Familiar City:

- Stabilize first: rub your hands.
- Take Flight: leap from a roof and feel the wind.
- Explore: land in a park, talk to a passerby.

Turning a Nightmare Friendly:

- **Acknowledge Fear:** remind yourself it's a dream.
- **Transform:** "I want this ominous hallway to become well-lit and safe."
- **Dialogue:** approach a threatening figure and ask, "Why are you here?"

These mini "dream scripts" help prepare your mind. Visualizing success in these scenarios can make them easier to enact when you're lucid.

4. Tips from Advanced Practitioners

Advanced dreamers consistently recommend these additional practices to strengthen lucidity and enhance experiences:

Verbal Clarity Commands: Many dreamers find the environment responds strongly to voice. State your desires clearly: "More color!" or "Increase brightness!"

- **Mindfulness in Dreaming:** Approach every lucid experience with calm curiosity rather than intense excitement. Excitement often triggers awakening, whereas mindfulness helps sustain dreams.
- **Use All Five Senses:** Taste the dream food, smell the air—engaging senses intensifies the dream's vividness and keeps you anchored.
- **Practice Gratitude:** Some oneironauts (explorers of dreams) report their lucidity lasts longer when they express positive emotion or thankfulness to the dream, fostering a "cooperative" atmosphere.

6. Key Takeaways

1. **Stabilize First:** Dream spinning, hand-rubbing, calm breathing—these steps ward off premature awakening.
2. **Shape the Environment:** You can summon new scenes, objects, or characters by focusing on intention and belief.
3. **Address Challenges Head-On:** Nightmares and false awakenings become opportunities for deeper self-awareness.
4. **Build Dream Confidence:** The more you practice and succeed, the easier it becomes to maintain control and reduce fear.

Exploring the lucid dream world is a highly personal journey. Some nights, you may prefer light-hearted adventures—flying, conjuring magical landscapes—while other times, you might confront deeper psychological themes or practice new skills. The core principle remains: in a lucid dream, you have the power to direct your experience. Let curiosity guide you, and remember: every new venture into lucidity is another chance to learn about your inner world.

CHAPTER 6: COMMON SYMBOLS AND DREAM THEMES

If Chapters 1 through 5 equip you with the tools to initiate and navigate lucid dreams, this chapter helps you **interpret** the content of those dreams. Dreams often contain powerful symbols, scenarios, or recurring themes—sometimes amusing, sometimes unsettling—each potentially holding meaning. Whether you're a firm believer in deep psychological underpinnings or you prefer a more literal approach, understanding dream symbolism can enrich your lucid experiences and help you gain personal insight.

1. Recurring Dream Elements to Watch For

1.1 Personal Dream Signs

Throughout your dream journal practice, you may find **certain elements that appear repeatedly**—a specific location (like your old school), an animal (like snakes or cats), or a reoccurring situation (like missing a flight). These are **personal dream signs**, unique to you, shaped by your memories, fears, or desires.

- **Emotional Resonance**: Personal signs typically carry strong emotions—either pleasant or unpleasant—and can be tied to unresolved feelings.
- **Lucidity Trigger**: Spotting a frequent dream sign is one of the most effective ways to *realize* you're dreaming (see Reality Checks in Chapter 4). When you notice "that same weird corridor" again, it's a chance to say, "Hold on

—am I dreaming?"

Neuroscientific research by **Matthew Walker** suggests dreams consolidate emotional experiences and memory patterns. Walker's work highlights that emotionally charged symbols or recurring themes (such as repeatedly dreaming of a stressful situation) frequently surface because they're connected to ongoing cognitive and emotional processing in the brain. Such patterns aren't random; they reflect deeper psychological processes, offering clues to unresolved issues or significant events in waking life.

Tip: Keep a dedicated page in your dream journal listing any symbol or scenario that pops up more than once a week or so. This helps you catch patterns quickly.

1.2 Universal or Common Themes

Psychologists, cultural anthropologists, and even casual dreamers have noted that certain dream motifs appear worldwide. While these themes aren't guaranteed to hold the same meaning for everyone, they often reflect broadly shared human experiences:

1. **Being Chased**: A universal anxiety dream; might symbolize avoidance of a problem or fear.
2. **Falling**: Often tied to stress or feeling out of control.
3. **Flying**: Can represent liberation, ambition, or the joy of transcending limitations.
4. **Naked in Public**: Usually linked to vulnerability or fear of exposure.
5. **Teeth Falling Out**: Commonly associated with concerns about appearance, aging, or losing control.
6. **Exams or Tests**: Might reflect performance anxiety or fear of not measuring up.
7. **House or Building**: Rooms and floors can symbolize different facets of your personality, memories, or mental "compartments."

8. **Car/Vehicle Issues**: Trouble steering or brakes failing can point to feeling powerless in waking life.

These themes show that, despite cultural differences, humans share many core anxieties and aspirations, which appear during dream states.

2. The Role of Personal and Collective Symbolism

2.1 Personal Symbolism

Dream interpretation is **highly personal**. For instance:

- A dog might represent loyalty and comfort to one dreamer, but fear or trauma to another.
- Water could symbolize peace or the subconscious to some, yet to a person who nearly drowned, it might evoke terror.

Because your memories and emotions are unique, it's crucial to think about **your own associations** when a symbol appears in your dream. Ask yourself: *"What does this image or situation mean to me personally?"*

2.2 Collective/Archetypal Symbolism

Swiss psychiatrist **Carl Jung** introduced the idea of *archetypes*: universal images or concepts that resonate across different cultures (e.g., the *Wise Old Man*, the *Shadow*, the *Hero*). Jung believed these patterns exist in a collective unconscious shared by humanity, which is why certain themes show up in myths, religions, and dreams worldwide.

Examples of archetypal figures or elements you might see in a lucid dream:

- **The Shadow**: A personification of aspects of yourself you'd rather not acknowledge.
- **The Guide** or **Wise Person**: An older, knowledgeable figure who offers advice—often interpreted as your deeper intuition.
- **The Anima/Animus**: An embodiment of one's

subconscious 'feminine' or 'masculine' qualities, respectively.

When you meet such figures in a lucid dream, you can engage them directly—ask questions, seek guidance—and see how they respond. Some dreamers report profound insights from these dialogues, regardless of whether they view them as literal archetypes or internal representations of the mind.

3. Decoding and Integrating Dream Messages

3.1 Practical Methods for Interpretation

1. **Ask "How Did I Feel?"**
   Emotions often guide interpretation. Were you anxious, peaceful, curious? Feelings can reveal whether a symbol represents stress, hope, or something else.

2. **Look for Real-World Triggers**
   Did something in your day remind you of the dream element? If you dreamed of an old friend, did you recently see a photo of them or hear their name? Such links can hint at why that symbol surfaced.

3. **Context Matters**
   Dream symbols rarely stand alone. If you see a snake in a bright, sunny garden, it could imply renewal; if it's chasing you through a dark hallway, it might reflect fear or betrayal.

4. **Experiment in Lucidity**
   In a lucid dream, you can **ask** a symbol (like a dream figure) what it means or why it appears. Some dreamers have in-dream conversations with, say, a giant crow that speaks or a mysterious robed figure who shares cryptic wisdom. Even if the answers feel bizarre, they may hold personal significance.

3.2 Journaling Techniques

- **Symbol Spotlight**: After writing your dream, list out any prominent or unusual symbols on a separate line.

Journal about what each might mean.

- **Compare Across Entries**: Look at past dreams to see if the same symbol reappears under similar emotional states or contexts.
- **Keyword Brainstorm**: Write the symbol in the center of a page and quickly jot down any words or memories you associate with it. This can uncover hidden links to your waking life.

3.3 Using Interpretation to Guide Personal Growth

- **Identify Unresolved Feelings**: Recurrent nightmares about being chased could reflect something specific you're avoiding in real life. Recognizing this pattern can motivate you to address the root cause.
- **Spot Hidden Desires**: Frequent dreams of flying might indicate a yearning for freedom or a break from routine. Acknowledging this can push you to seek more independence or creativity in daily life.
- **Fuel Creative Projects**: If you're a writer, artist, or musician, analyzing dream symbols can inspire new storylines, characters, or designs.

4. Lucid Dream Work: Engaging Symbols on the Spot

When you're **lucid**, you have a unique opportunity to investigate symbolism in real-time. For instance, you see a peculiar door in your dream—open it intentionally. If a giant bird appears, **ask** it: *"Why are you here?"* You might get a surprising answer. Even if the response seems nonsensical, it often triggers an emotional or intuitive insight that becomes clearer upon waking.

- **Conscious Transformation**: If you encounter a symbol that frightens you (like a ferocious lion), see if you can change it. Transform the lion into a friendly creature or guide. This can shift your emotional response, teaching your mind that the fear is manageable or may represent a personal challenge you can overcome.

- **Summon Dream Guides**: Some experienced lucid dreamers specifically call upon a 'dream guide' or 'inner wisdom' figure to discuss recurring symbols, effectively having a conversation with their subconscious.

5. Cultural and Shared Symbolism Caveat

It's worth noting that some symbols carry strong cultural connotations—like dragons in Chinese culture symbolizing power and fortune, versus Western lore where dragons might be fearsome enemies. If you find a symbol from another culture appearing in your dream, it might reflect that culture's influence on your psyche (perhaps through media or heritage), or your personal relationship with it.

Similarly, so-called "dream dictionaries" can offer interesting perspectives but shouldn't be taken as universal truths. Any interpretation must be balanced against your own experiences and feelings.

6. Practical Example: Symbol Analysis Walk-Through

Let's consider a hypothetical dream scenario:

Dream:
You're in a dimly lit library, and a black cat jumps onto a table. It stares at you, then darts away. You chase it down endless aisles of books but never catch it. Finally, it disappears behind a door marked with a glowing moon symbol.

- **Initial Emotional Tone**: Possibly curiosity or mild frustration (chasing the cat).
- **Key Symbols**:
    - **Library**: Knowledge, learning, exploration.
    - **Black Cat**: Could represent intuition, mystery, or unpredictability.
    - **Glowing Moon Symbol**: Maybe something hidden in your subconscious, or a connection to nighttime intuition.
- **Personal Associations**: If you like cats, this might

not feel ominous; if you fear them, it might indicate something you're reluctant to face. Maybe you spent the day reading an article about superstitions involving black cats.

- **Possible Interpretation**: A part of you is seeking knowledge (library) or deeper subconscious insights (moon), yet you feel you can't quite "catch" it. The black cat might represent a hidden instinct or fear that you need to approach differently in waking life.

If Lucid:

During the chase, you become lucid and realize you're dreaming. You could:

- Call out to the cat, "Stop—I want to talk!"
- Open the moon-marked door intentionally, expecting answers on the other side.
- Use a **grounding technique** if the dream becomes unstable.
- Upon waking, reflect on any new information or emotional shifts from your lucid interaction.

7. Final Thoughts on Symbols and Themes

- **No One-Size-Fits-All**: The same symbol can have vastly different meanings between two people. Honor your personal perspective.
- **Symbols Evolve Over Time**: As you change, your dream symbols may transform. A spider that once symbolized fear might later appear friendly if you've overcome a related issue.
- **Stay Curious, Not Rigid**: Approach dream interpretation with openness. Dreams blend memory, emotion, and imagination; their logic is less linear than waking life.

Interpreting dream symbols can be a fun, enlightening process rather than a riddle with a single right answer. By blending personal reflection, cultural knowledge, and—when lucid—direct interaction, you'll extract deeper meaning from the images your mind crafts each night.

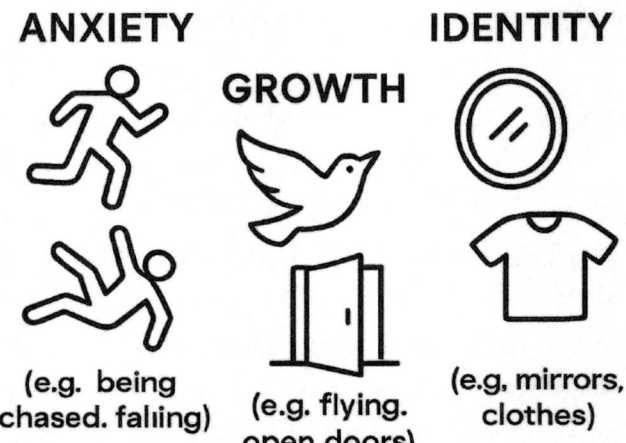

CHAPTER 7: DEEPENING YOUR LUCID DREAM PRACTICE

By now, you've learned how to achieve lucidity, navigate dreamscapes, and interpret dream symbols. This chapter will help you take your lucid dreaming further—moving beyond simply experiencing lucid dreams into using them for personal growth, healing, creativity, and exploring consciousness itself.

Advanced practices involve integrating meditation, mindfulness, and intentional dream tasks. These methods not only enhance your lucid dreaming abilities but can profoundly influence your waking life.

---

1. Meditation and Mindfulness for Lucid Dreaming

Research shows that meditation enhances cognitive awareness, self-reflection, and emotional stability—exactly the skills required for successful lucid dreaming. Studies by Baird et al. (2019) and Stumbrys et al. (2015) demonstrated that regular meditation significantly enhances lucid dream frequency. Participants practicing mindfulness showed increased lucidity due to improved metacognitive abilities—awareness of their own thinking processes within dreams.

1.1 How Meditation Enhances Lucidity:

- **Improved Mindfulness**: Regular meditation strengthens your capacity to remain aware, a key to lucidity.
- **Emotional Stability**: Meditation helps manage excitement or anxiety, preventing early awakening from lucidity.
- **Enhanced Recall**: Mindfulness meditation increases your ability to remember dreams clearly.

Practical Mindfulness Exercises:

- **Daily Mindfulness Check-ins**: Throughout your day, pause regularly and ask yourself, "Am I dreaming?" Feel your feet on the ground, notice sensory details, and perform reality checks mindfully.
- **Mindful Breathing (Daytime and Bedtime)**: Spend 5–10 minutes per day focusing on your breathing. This practice trains your mind to remain anchored in the present, enhancing clarity during dreams.
- **Visualization Meditations**: Before bed, visualize becoming lucid in a dream. Regularly practicing this creates mental habits that transfer easily into sleep.

2. Lucid Dreaming for Therapeutic Purposes

Scientific studies, including those conducted by Denholm Aspy and Ursula Voss, indicate lucid dreaming can be beneficial for mental health, helping alleviate anxiety, nightmares, and even PTSD symptoms. Ursula Voss's research emphasizes lucid dreaming's therapeutic potential, particularly her findings on using lucid dreams to manage nightmares and PTSD-related symptoms. In clinical contexts, lucid dreaming significantly reduced traumatic nightmare occurrences and improved emotional regulation.

2.1 Overcoming Nightmares:

Lucid dreaming lets you confront and reshape nightmares directly, transforming fear into empowerment:

- **Face Your Fears Directly**: Approach a threatening dream character and calmly engage or command it to leave.
- **Rewrite Your Narrative**: Change the dream's outcome consciously, turning danger into triumph or fear into acceptance.

Clinical trials show lucid dreamers experience fewer recurring nightmares, higher emotional resilience, and better overall sleep quality.

2.2 Healing Past Trauma:

Lucid dreams provide a safe space to revisit past experiences. You control the dream and can consciously reshape memories or emotional responses:

- **Dialoguing with Dream Characters**: Have open conversations with representations of people involved in trauma to foster emotional resolution.
- **Symbolic Healing Rituals**: In lucid dreams, perform symbolic acts of closure—such as letting go of an object representing pain or trauma.

Lucid dream therapy can complement traditional counseling, providing profound internal resolution.

3. Creative Problem-Solving and Artistic Inspiration

Historical and contemporary examples (such as Salvador Dalí's "hypnagogic" dreaming method) find strong support in neuroscientific research by Erlacher and Schredl (2010), indicating that lucid dream rehearsal effectively enhances creative problem-solving and performance skills. This phenomenon closely mirrors the familiar experience of stepping away from a challenging problem during the day—only for the solution to suddenly emerge seemingly "out of nowhere." Similarly, lucid dreaming can tap into your subconscious creativity, unlocking ideas and insights that your waking, focused mind might overlook.

3.1 Why Lucid Dreams Boost Creativity:

- **Limitless Possibilities**: In lucid dreams, physical laws are irrelevant. Explore impossible scenarios that inspire original ideas.
- **Direct Communication with Your Subconscious**: Lucid dreams allow you to consciously interact with your deepest creative insights.

3.2 Techniques for Creative Dreaming:

- **Summon Creative Guides**: Consciously invite dream characters representing creativity, such as admired artists or imaginary mentors, and ask for inspiration.
- **Experiment Freely**: If you're stuck in a creative block, use lucid dreams to try new approaches without judgment or limits.
- **Artistic Rehearsal**: Practice performances, speeches, or techniques within the dream to boost confidence and refine skills.

Throughout history, artists and inventors, including Salvador Dalí and Nikola Tesla, have credited dreams with groundbreaking ideas. Lucid dreaming takes this even further by placing you consciously at the creative helm.

4. Lucid Dreaming for Skill Improvement

Erlacher's research (2017) documented measurable improvements in motor skills following lucid dream rehearsal. Athletes who practiced tasks during lucid dreams showed enhanced real-world performance, demonstrating neurological transfer from dream experiences to waking states.

4.1 Sports and Motor Skills:

- Practice your sport—whether it's skiing, martial arts, or dancing—in your lucid dreams, improving your technique and confidence without physical fatigue or

injury risk.
- Athletes using lucid dream rehearsal report measurable improvements in confidence and muscle memory.

4.2 Social and Emotional Skills:
- Safely rehearse challenging social scenarios (like public speaking or difficult conversations), building confidence and social competence.
- Test emotional responses to stressful situations, preparing yourself psychologically for real-world challenges.

5. Exploring Consciousness and Spirituality

Beyond therapeutic and creative uses, lucid dreams offer unique opportunities for spiritual exploration and understanding consciousness.

5.1 Dream Yoga and Conscious Exploration:

The Tibetan tradition of dream yoga treats lucid dreaming as a tool for spiritual insight and understanding the nature of reality.

- **Meditation within Dreams**: Meditate consciously in a lucid dream to achieve profound inner clarity or insights.
- **Exploring Self and Identity**: Engage dream figures in philosophical discussions about identity, self-awareness, or the nature of reality, creating powerful moments of self-understanding.

5.2 Connecting to Inner Wisdom:
- Many lucid dreamers report meeting "dream guides," symbolic figures representing intuition or higher wisdom.
- Directly asking these guides questions about life purpose or decisions can result in surprising clarity and insight.

6. Advanced Dream Control Techniques

For experienced lucid dreamers, dream control moves beyond simple scene creation to deeper manipulation and exploration.

6.1 Layered Lucidity:

- **Dream Within a Dream**: Deliberately enter deeper layers of dreams (akin to popular depictions in movies) to further explore consciousness.
- This advanced technique allows exploration of multiple dimensions of self-awareness simultaneously.

6.2 Time Dilation:

- Experimenting with altering your perception of time within a dream. Some lucid dreamers report seemingly experiencing days within a single night's dream.
- Useful for extended creative work, problem-solving, or prolonged exploration.

7. Building a Lucid Dreaming Lifestyle

To sustain deepened lucid practice:

- **Consistency is Key**: Regular meditation, dream journaling, and reality checks build a solid foundation.
- **Community Support**: Engage in forums or groups to share experiences, gain fresh techniques, and remain motivated.
- **Continued Learning**: Regularly explore new research, ideas, and methods to continuously enrich your practice.

8. Integrating Lucid Dream Insights into Waking Life

After waking:

- Immediately journal significant insights or solutions discovered in dreams.
- Reflect regularly on the connections between dream experiences and waking-life situations.

- Actively integrate dream insights—apply creative breakthroughs or therapeutic revelations to your daily activities and personal growth.

9. Precautions and Responsible Dreaming

As you deepen your lucid dreaming:

- Maintain healthy sleep hygiene. Avoid excessive disruption of sleep cycles.
- Be cautious with dream supplements or substances, approaching them with careful research and moderation.
- Remember that lucid dreams are an addition to, not a substitute for, professional therapeutic support when needed.

Chapter 7: Key Takeaways

- **Meditation and mindfulness** significantly amplify lucid dream practice and cognitive awareness.
- Lucid dreaming can offer powerful tools for **therapy**, reducing anxiety, nightmares, and trauma symptoms.
- **Creativity and skill practice** within lucid dreams can meaningfully enhance real-world performance and innovation.
- Advanced lucid dreaming methods, including dream yoga and consciousness exploration, open profound personal insights.
- **Integration and responsible practice** ensure your lucid dream experiences enhance—not disrupt—your overall well-being.

CHAPTER 8: TROUBLESHOOTING & FAQS

Even experienced lucid dreamers encounter occasional challenges or barriers. This chapter provides clear, practical guidance to address common issues, answer frequently asked questions, and maintain steady progress toward lucid dreaming mastery.

Troubleshooting Common Challenges

1. "I Keep Waking Up Too Quickly After Becoming Lucid."

This issue often arises from excitement or anxiety upon realizing you're dreaming.

Solutions:

- **Use grounding techniques immediately (rubbing hands, spinning, verbal commands), proven by LaBerge's research to prolong dreams.**
- **Remain calm and breathe slowly, reminding yourself you have plenty of time to explore.**
- **Practice mindfulness daily, as regular meditation helps regulate emotional responses, reducing premature awakenings.**

2. "I'm Having Trouble Becoming Lucid Consistently."

Lucidity can fluctuate, especially if daily habits slip or your sleep routine is inconsistent.

Solutions:

- Increase daily reality checks and mindfulness. Be deliberate, questioning reality often.
- Maintain consistent sleep patterns. Irregular sleep schedules disrupt REM cycles, reducing lucid dream frequency.
- Combine techniques (e.g., WBTB + MILD or reality checks), significantly increasing success rates (Aspy, 2017).

3. "Reality Checks Don't Work for Me in Dreams."

Occasionally, dreamers find reality checks unreliable if performed without mindfulness.

Solutions:

- Perform reality checks mindfully, genuinely questioning reality rather than doing them automatically.
- Switch techniques if your current checks don't resonate. If the finger-count method isn't effective, try the nose-pinch or text-reading test instead.
- Strengthen prospective memory (remembering future intentions) by clearly visualizing becoming lucid whenever you perform a check.

5. "I Have False Awakenings Often.
6. "False awakenings—dreaming you've woken up—can cause confusion or frustration.

Solutions:

- Always reality-check when waking, making it a habit each morning or after nighttime awakenings.
- Embrace false awakenings as opportunities. Each provides another chance to achieve lucidity.

5. "My Dreams Aren't Vivid Enough."

Low dream clarity can hinder recognition of dream signs and lucidity triggers.

Solutions:

- Increase dream recall through consistent journaling. Clearer recall enhances vividness.
- Consider dream-enhancing techniques, such as meditation, visualization, or dietary adjustments (reducing caffeine and alcohol).
- Sleep longer and deeper. Improving sleep hygiene directly enhances dream vividness and recall quality.

6. "I'm Experiencing Sleep Paralysis Frequently."

Sleep paralysis, a feeling of being unable to move upon waking or falling asleep, often comes with vivid sensations.

Solutions:

- Understand sleep paralysis as harmless and temporary. Simply recognizing it reduces anxiety.
- Try gently moving a small body part, like fingers or toes, to ease out of paralysis gradually.
- Reduce occurrences by managing stress, avoiding irregular sleep schedules, and maintaining good sleep hygiene.

Frequently Asked Questions (FAQs)

Q: "Is Lucid Dreaming Safe?"
A: Yes, lucid dreaming is generally safe and beneficial. Research consistently shows positive psychological effects, like reduced nightmares and anxiety. Practice responsibly and maintain healthy sleep habits.

Q: "Can I Get Stuck in a Lucid Dream?"
A: No. Lucid dreams always naturally end. While "false awakenings" can feel confusing, you cannot get permanently trapped. Regular reality checks easily resolve false awakenings.

Q: "Can Lucid Dreaming Make Me Tired?"
A: Usually not, especially if you maintain good sleep hygiene. However, methods like WBTB may cause temporary fatigue if you disrupt sleep excessively. Balance practice with adequate rest.

Q: "Is Lucid Dreaming Suitable for Everyone?"
A: Most people can benefit from lucid dreaming. However, those experiencing certain mental health conditions or sleep disorders should consult medical professionals before extensive practice.

Q: "Why Do My Reality Checks Fail in Dreams?"
A: Typically, it's due to performing them automatically without mindful questioning. Always actively question your reality while performing checks during the day to ensure effectiveness in dreams.

Advanced Troubleshooting & Tips from Experts

- "I'm Lucid, but I Struggle to Control the Dream."
  - Begin with small, confident changes (like altering minor objects). Gradually build confidence for larger transformations. Lucid control improves significantly with practice.
- "How Can I Lucid Dream More Often?"
  - Combine daily mindfulness meditation, regular reality checking, and the WBTB + MILD technique. Denholm Aspy's extensive studies suggest this combination yields higher success rates.
- "What If I Encounter Scary or Uncomfortable Situations?"
  - Lucid dreaming allows safe confrontation. Face these situations directly and transform or dialogue with frightening elements. Research (Spoormaker & van den Bout, 2006) confirms this significantly reduces fear responses and nightmares over time.

Creating a Consistent Lucid Dreaming Routine

Lucid dreaming thrives on consistency and patience:

- **Daily Habits:**
    - Perform mindful reality checks (5-10 daily).
    - Journal dreams immediately upon waking.
    - Engage in brief mindfulness meditation or breathing exercises daily.
- **Nightly Practices:**
    - Set clear lucid intentions before sleeping.
    - Regularly practice MILD or WBTB methods several nights per week.
- **Weekly Check-ins:**
    - Review your dream journal for recurring themes or progress.
    - Adapt methods based on what consistently works best.

Key Takeaways (Chapter 8):

- **Regularly perform mindful reality checks to improve effectiveness.**
- **Prioritize consistent sleep schedules and good sleep hygiene to enhance dream vividness and lucidity frequency.**
- **Utilize proven techniques (WBTB, MILD) based on research to consistently achieve lucidity.**
- **Embrace challenges, such as nightmares and false awakenings, as opportunities for growth rather than setbacks.**
- **Maintain a balanced approach, recognizing lucid dreaming as a skill developed gradually through patience and persistence.**

CHAPTER 9: INTEGRATING LUCID DREAMS INTO DAILY LIFE

Lucid dreaming isn't just a fascinating nighttime adventure—it's a powerful tool that can significantly enrich your daily life. By consciously integrating insights and experiences from your dreams into waking reality, you can boost creativity, accelerate personal growth, resolve real-world problems, and enhance emotional well-being.

In this chapter, we'll explore practical ways to bridge your dream world with your waking life, based on established psychological research and real-world success stories.

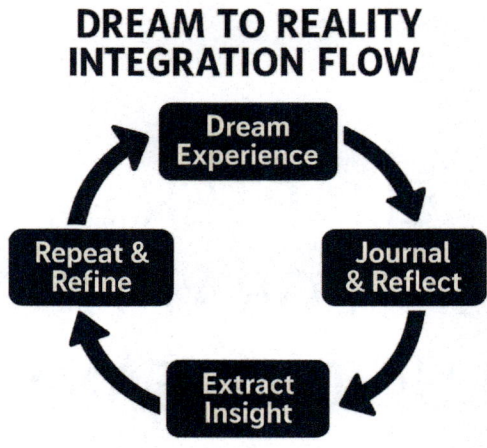

1. Using Lucid Dreams for Problem-Solving and Decision-Making

Lucid dreaming provides direct access to your subconscious mind, a wellspring of ideas and insights often hidden during waking life.

Practical Techniques:

- **Problem Rehearsal:**
  When facing a challenging issue, consciously enter a lucid dream intending to explore solutions. Visualize or summon relevant scenarios, experimenting freely without limitations.

- **Seeking Advice from Dream Figures:**
  Interact directly with dream characters. Ask specific questions like, "What's the best way forward?" The responses—symbolic or direct—often provide unexpected clarity.

- **Post-Dream Reflection:**
  Upon awakening, immediately write down dream insights and evaluate their practical applicability. Consider these insights with a curious and open mindset.

Real-World Application:

Many inventors, including historical figures like Thomas Edison and contemporary creatives, have credited dreams with groundbreaking ideas. Neuroscience research by Erlacher and Schredl (2010) confirms that dream-rehearsed solutions significantly improve real-life creative problem-solving.

2. Enhancing Creativity and Innovation

Your dream environment, free from conventional constraints, encourages innovative thinking and limitless imagination.

How Lucid Dreams Boost Creativity:

- Idea Incubation:
  Before bed, clearly set an intention (e.g., "Tonight, I'll explore a new idea for my book"). Allow the dream to generate scenarios, symbolism, or direct inspiration.
- Artistic Experimentation:
  Lucidly practice your art, music, writing, or performance in your dream. Experiment without fear of judgment or failure, unlocking new approaches and insights.
- Symbolic Creativity:
  Pay close attention to symbols or unusual imagery within lucid dreams. They frequently provide unexpected inspirations for creative projects.

Real-Life Example:

Artists like Salvador Dalí famously utilized dream states (hypnagogic imagery) to inspire iconic works. Modern research confirms that this approach significantly enhances creative breakthroughs.

3. Emotional and Psychological Growth

Lucid dreaming provides a safe platform to confront fears, explore hidden emotions, and enhance emotional resilience.

Therapeutic Techniques:

- **Facing Emotional Challenges:**
  Intentionally summon or engage with symbols of emotional difficulty (e.g., confronting fears or past traumas). Studies (Spoormaker & van den Bout, 2006) confirm this directly reduces waking anxiety.

- **Practicing Assertiveness and Confidence:**
  Safely rehearse challenging social or professional interactions in lucid dreams, gradually boosting real-life confidence.

- **Rewriting Emotional Narratives:**
  If you frequently experience stressful or negative dreams, consciously re-enter them lucidly and rewrite the outcome positively, significantly shifting emotional associations.

Supporting Research:

Clinical studies strongly support lucid dreaming as a therapeutic method for managing anxiety, PTSD, and stress-related disorders, indicating improved emotional stability and resilience.

4. Skill Development Through Lucid Dream Practice

Your brain reacts similarly to imagined actions in dreams as it does to physical practice, making lucid dreaming a potent skill-building tool.

Practical Skill-Building Methods:

- **Motor Skills and Sports:**
  Practice specific physical activities (martial arts, sports techniques, dance moves) lucidly, improving muscle memory and confidence without physical strain or injury risk.

- **Public Speaking and Social Skills:**
  Rehearse speeches, presentations, or difficult conversations lucidly, improving clarity, reducing anxiety, and enhancing performance.

- **Creative Arts:**
  Experiment creatively in dreams to refine ideas or techniques in music, writing, painting, or other arts.

Scientific Validation:

Erlacher (2017) demonstrated that lucid dream rehearsal directly improved waking-life performance, particularly in motor skills, affirming the power of lucid dreaming for practical skill development.

5. Spiritual Growth and Insight

For those inclined, lucid dreaming offers opportunities for deep introspection, spiritual exploration, and profound personal insights.

Methods for Spiritual Exploration:

- **Dream Meditation:**
  Engage in meditation within the lucid dream to explore deep consciousness or spiritual insight.

- **Meeting Dream Guides:**
  Consciously summon spiritual or wisdom figures, dialoguing about personal purpose, decisions, or existential questions.

- **Exploring Consciousness:**
  Investigate the nature of identity and self-awareness by observing and interacting mindfully with dream environments and characters.

6. Practical Integration Techniques for Daily Life

Meaningful integration requires deliberate post-dream reflection and real-world application.

Integration Methods:

- **Dream Journal Reviews:**
  Regularly read back through your dream journal, highlighting significant insights or recurring themes and consciously applying them to daily decisions or

challenges.

- **Actionable Goal Setting:**
  Translate insights into clear, actionable waking-life goals (e.g., pursuing a new hobby, addressing relationship issues, or making career changes).
- **Mindful Reflection and Meditation:**
  Take time each morning to reflect on dream experiences, contemplating lessons learned and integrating these consciously into your mindset for the day.

7. Creating a Lucid Lifestyle—Consistency and Habit Building

Maintaining a consistent, balanced approach is key to integrating lucid dreaming effectively into daily life.

Recommended Daily Habits:

- Perform mindful reality checks regularly.
- Maintain daily meditation or mindfulness practice to enhance overall awareness.
- Journaling consistently upon waking to strengthen recall and emotional processing.

Long-term Integration Habits:

- Regularly review dream insights, connecting them consciously to personal growth.
- Share and discuss dream experiences with a community or group, reinforcing integration and motivation.

8. Overcoming Integration Challenges

Sometimes applying dream insights to waking life may feel unclear or difficult.

Solutions to Common Challenges:

- **Vague Dreams:**
  If dream symbolism feels confusing, engage

consciously in lucid dreams—asking dream characters directly for clarity or interpreting their answers intuitively upon waking.

- Forgetfulness:
  Prioritize immediate dream journaling and routine reflection to reinforce memory and insights.
- Resistance to Change:
  If dream insights challenge your comfort zone, integrate them gradually into small, manageable actions to ease into meaningful growth.

Key Takeaways (Chapter 9):

- **Lucid dreaming significantly enhances problem-solving, creativity, emotional resilience, and skill development, with strong backing from scientific research.**
- **Practical integration involves mindful reflection, actionable goals, and regular application of insights into daily life.**
- **Maintaining a consistent, mindful approach ensures your dream experiences positively enrich your waking reality, fostering meaningful personal growth and transformation.**

CHAPTER 10: FINAL REFLECTIONS & NEXT STEPS

Congratulations on completing your journey through the world of lucid dreaming! You've learned foundational methods, explored advanced techniques, interpreted dream symbolism, and discovered practical ways to integrate lucid dreaming into your daily life. As you conclude this book, consider this chapter your personal guide for continued growth, reflection, and deeper exploration into the transformative potential of lucid dreaming.

Reflecting on Your Lucid Dreaming Journey

Take a moment to appreciate how far you've come. Whether you've experienced your first lucid dream or dramatically enhanced your dreaming abilities, each step represents significant progress. Reflecting on your achievements helps solidify your learning and motivates ongoing practice.

Reflective Prompts:

- What was your most meaningful lucid dreaming experience?
Reflect on why it stood out and what insights or emotions it revealed.
- Which induction methods resonated most strongly with you?
Reflecting on this helps you tailor your practice

effectively in the future.
- Have your dreams revealed recurring symbols or themes?
Consider their potential meanings and how they might guide future self-exploration.

Core Insights from This Book

Before looking ahead, let's briefly recap the core insights you've gained:

1. **Lucid Dreaming is Learnable and Practical:**
   Scientific research consistently demonstrates lucid dreaming's practical applications—from nightmare management and emotional healing to enhanced creativity and improved skills.

2. **Consistency and Mindfulness are Essential:**
   Daily mindfulness, reality checking, meditation, and regular dream journaling reliably boost lucid dreaming success rates.

3. **Personal Symbolism and Interpretation:**
   Dreams speak uniquely to your subconscious. Understanding personal symbolism significantly enhances your self-awareness and emotional growth.

4. **Integration Transforms Dreams into Real-World Growth:**
   Consciously applying dream insights to waking life provides tangible emotional, creative, and personal development.

Continued Growth: Strategies for Long-Term Lucidity

Lucid dreaming, like any skill, continues to develop with sustained practice and curiosity. Consider these strategies for lifelong growth:

- **Maintain a Dream Journal Long-Term:**
  Keeping consistent records ensures ongoing insight, enhances recall, and helps spot evolving themes or

symbolism.
- **Regular Mindfulness and Meditation:**
  Mindfulness practices continuously improve dream clarity, lucidity frequency, and overall psychological well-being.
- **Advanced Dream Goals:**
  Set evolving goals—such as mastering advanced lucid techniques (time dilation, dream yoga) or exploring deeper self-awareness through dream interactions.

Deepening Your Practice with Advanced Techniques

Now that you've mastered the basics, consider these exciting advanced practices:

- **Dream Yoga and Consciousness Exploration:**
  Dive deeper into understanding the nature of consciousness, identity, and spiritual insight through meditation and intentional dream exploration.
- **Creative Mastery:**
  Intentionally pursue complex creative projects within lucid dreams, using this powerful tool for artistic or professional breakthroughs.
- **Therapeutic and Healing Practices:**
  Utilize lucid dreaming intentionally for deep emotional healing, trauma recovery, and personal resilience, guided by scientific research demonstrating clear therapeutic benefits.

Troubleshooting and Adaptation for Ongoing Success

Throughout your journey, challenges will naturally arise. Use these simple strategies to troubleshoot effectively:

- **Revisit Techniques Regularly:**
  If lucidity drops off, return to foundational methods (WBTB, MILD, mindful reality checks) to regain consistency.

- **Join a Lucid Dreaming Community:**
  Engaging regularly with others provides ongoing motivation, support, and fresh ideas for continued growth.
- **Stay Updated on Lucid Dreaming Research:**
  Regularly exploring new scientific findings or innovations in lucid dreaming keeps your practice fresh, evidence-based, and inspiring.

Recommended Resources for Lifelong Learning

To sustain and enhance your lucid dreaming journey, explore these valuable resources:

- **The Lucidity Institute:**
  Founded by Stephen LaBerge, it offers research updates, training workshops, and helpful guidance (www.lucidity.com).
- **Dream Research:**
  Follow researchers like Denholm Aspy, Ursula Voss, and Matthew Walker, whose work continually expands scientific understanding of dreams and consciousness.
- **Lucid Dreaming Communities and Forums:**
  Engage with platforms such as Reddit's r/LucidDreaming or specialized groups that regularly share experiences, tips, and motivation.
- **Further Reading and Courses:**
  Books such as *Exploring the World of Lucid Dreaming* by Stephen LaBerge and courses from reputable platforms provide structured, ongoing support.

Encouragement and Inspiration for Your Journey Ahead

Your exploration of lucid dreaming can be as limitless as the dreams themselves. Remember:

- **Every lucid dream is a valuable opportunity:**
  Each experience, regardless of length or complexity, provides insight into your inner world.

- **Be patient, persistent, and curious:**
  Lucid dreaming rewards consistent, gentle practice. Be open to new ideas, adjustments, and creative explorations.

- **Allow dreams to inspire your waking life:**
  Regularly reflect on your experiences and consciously integrate dream insights into your daily routine. This will continually enrich your personal growth, creativity, and emotional well-being.

Final Thoughts

Lucid dreaming bridges the conscious and subconscious, transforming ordinary sleep into powerful personal exploration. As you move forward, maintain curiosity, openness, and intentional practice. The tools and insights you've acquired are lifelong assets for ongoing self-discovery, emotional healing, creative expression, and spiritual exploration.

Remember, the adventure doesn't end here—every night offers another chance to step into a lucid dream and unlock its vast potential.

Sweet dreams, lucid explorer!

Your Next Steps Checklist:

- **Continue daily dream journaling.**
- **Maintain mindful reality checks and meditation practices.**
- **Join a lucid dreaming community for ongoing inspiration.**
- **Set and revisit lucid dreaming goals regularly.**
- **Explore advanced dream techniques and spiritual insights.**
- **Regularly integrate dream lessons into your daily life.**
- **Stay informed on scientific research and**

developments.

Thank you for letting me guide you through your lucid dreaming journey—may it continually enrich and inspire every aspect of your waking life!

References and Resources

Below are references and recommended resources that informed and supported the content throughout this book. Use these to further explore and deepen your lucid dreaming practice.

Scientific Studies & Research

- Aspy, Denholm (2017).
  Reality Testing and the Mnemonic Induction of Lucid Dreams: Findings from the National Australian Lucid Dream Induction Study. Dreaming, 27(3), 206–231.
  https://doi.org/10.1037/drm0000059

- Baird, Benjamin, et al. (2019).
  Increased Lucid Dream Frequency in Long-term Meditators but not Following Mindfulness-based Stress Reduction Training. Psychology of Consciousness: Theory, Research, and Practice, 6(1), 40–54.
  https://doi.org/10.1037/cns0000176

- Erlacher, Daniel & Schredl, Michael (2010).
  Practicing a Motor Task in a Lucid Dream Enhances Subsequent Performance: A Pilot Study. The Sport Psychologist, 24(2), 157–167.
  https://doi.org/10.1123/tsp.24.2.157

- Erlacher, Daniel (2017).
  Motor Learning in Lucid Dreams. Journal of Lucid Dreaming Research, 1(1), 1–13.

- LaBerge, Stephen (1985).
  Lucid Dreaming: The Power of Being Awake and Aware in Your Dreams. New York: Ballantine Books.

- Spoormaker, Victor & van den Bout, Jan (2006).
  Lucid Dreaming Treatment for Nightmares: A Pilot Study.

- Psychotherapy and Psychosomatics, 75(6), 389–394.
  https://doi.org/10.1159/000095446
- Stumbrys, Tadas, Erlacher, Daniel & Malinowski, Peter (2015).
  Meta-Awareness During Day and Night: The Relationship Between Mindfulness and Lucid Dreaming. Imagination, Cognition and Personality, 34(4), 415–433.
  https://doi.org/10.1177/0276236615572594
- Voss, Ursula, et al. (2014).
  Induction of Self-awareness in Dreams through Frontal Low Current Stimulation of Gamma Activity. Nature Neuroscience, 17(6), 810–812.
  https://doi.org/10.1038/nn.3719
- Walker, Matthew (2017).
  Why We Sleep: Unlocking the Power of Sleep and Dreams. Scribner Publishing.

Foundational Psychology and Archetypes

- Jung, Carl Gustav (1969).
  The Archetypes and the Collective Unconscious. (Collected Works of C.G. Jung, Vol. 9, Part 1). Princeton University Press.

Recommended Books & Reading

- LaBerge, Stephen & Rheingold, Howard (1991).
  Exploring the World of Lucid Dreaming. New York: Ballantine Books.
- Wallace, Alan (2012).
  Dreaming Yourself Awake: Lucid Dreaming and Tibetan Dream Yoga for Insight and Transformation. Shambhala Publications.

Online Resources and Communities

- Lucidity Institute (Stephen LaBerge):
  Practical information, research updates, workshops, and tools.

https://www.lucidity.com

- **Reddit Lucid Dreaming Community:**
  Engaged online forum sharing experiences, tips, and support.
  https://www.reddit.com/r/LucidDreaming

Your Companion Dream Journals

- **Dream Journal: Dream Relax Reflect Remember Embrace**
  https://amzn.to/3DXO3bb

- **Dream Journal: Dream Relax Reflect Remember Embrace (Alternative Edition)**
  https://amzn.to/4i3wmFi

🌙 Epilogue: A Personal Message

As we reach the conclusion of our lucid dreaming journey together, I'd like to sincerely thank you for joining me in exploring the extraordinary world of lucid dreaming. For me, lucid dreaming has been transformative—sparking creativity, providing emotional healing, and opening the door to profound self-discovery.

My hope is that you continue to explore your dreams with curiosity and courage, using each night as an opportunity for new adventures and insights. Remember that the beauty of lucid dreaming lies in its endless potential. Wherever your dreams take you next, trust in your ability to learn, grow, and thrive.

Thank you for allowing me to be a part of your journey. Wishing you clarity, wisdom, and many incredible dreams ahead!

Sweet dreams, fellow dreamer!

🌙 Quick Reference Guide

Here's a concise summary of key practices from this book to support your ongoing lucid dreaming adventures:

Daily Practices:

- **Reality Checks:**
  Perform 5–10 mindful checks daily, genuinely questioning your reality.
- **Dream Journaling:**
  Immediately record your dreams upon waking each morning to enhance recall and insight.
- **Meditation and Mindfulness:**
  Dedicate 5–10 minutes daily to meditation or mindfulness exercises to boost awareness and lucidity.

Lucid Dream Induction:

- **Reality Checks & Dream Signs:**
  Regularly check reality when encountering recurring symbols or dream signs.
- **Mnemonic Induction (MILD):**
  Clearly set your intention to become lucid before sleeping, visualizing recognition of dream signs.
- **Wake Back to Bed (WBTB):**
  Briefly wake after 4–6 hours of sleep; stay awake briefly before returning to sleep, combining with MILD or WILD techniques.

Dream Stabilization:

- **Spinning in Place / Rubbing Hands:**
  Use these grounding techniques immediately when lucidity occurs to prolong your dream.
- **Verbal Commands:**
  Clearly state commands within the dream, like "Increase clarity" or "I remain lucid," to stabilize and control your experience.

Integrating Dream Insights:

- Regularly review your dream journal, identify themes, and consciously apply insights to your daily life for

ongoing growth.

Coming Soon

Thank you for exploring lucid dreaming with me! I'm excited to share that there are more resources and tools coming your way soon, designed to deepen your dream experiences and enrich your life even further:

- Interpreting Dreams and Symbols
  A clear and practical guide to help you uncover hidden meanings and understand the deeper messages within your dreams.
- Dream Journals
  Beautifully crafted journals designed specifically to improve dream recall and lucidity—perfect companions for your nightly adventures.
- Comprehensive Dream App
  A user-friendly app offering instant dream meanings, personalized insights, and guidance to support your ongoing lucid dreaming practice.

Let's Stay Connected!

I'd love to continue supporting your lucid dreaming journey. Here are several ways we can stay connected:

Explore My Dream Journals:

- **Dream Journal: Dream Relax Reflect Remember Embrace**
- **Dream Journal: Dream Relax Reflect Remember Embrace (Alternative Edition)**

Visit My Website: For updates and upcoming resources

https://dreamandbelieve.my.canva.site/

Join the Community:

- **Join the mailing list for ongoing resources, special offers, and updates:**

dreamandbelieve@myyahoo.com

Thank you again for allowing me to guide you. May your lucid dreaming practice enrich your life deeply, bringing clarity, creativity, and lasting personal growth.

Happy dreaming, and I hope to hear from you soon!

ABOUT THE AUTHOR

Marc Reynolds

I'm a writer, creative thinker, and problem solver with a passion for science fiction, storytelling, and exploring new ideas. My love for speculative fiction, from Star Trek to The Three-Body Problem, has inspired me to craft my own stories—blending technology, human nature, and the unknown.

Beyond writing, I enjoy creating tools and resources that help people engage with their thoughts, whether through journaling, analysis, or simply sparking curiosity. With a background in software testing and automation, I have a structured approach to creativity, balancing logic with imagination.

For me, writing is about more than just telling a story—it's about building worlds, asking big questions, and discovering new perspectives. Whether it's fiction, journaling, or creative projects, I'm always looking for ways to make ideas come to life.

BOOKS BY THIS AUTHOR

Dream Journal: Dream Relax Reflect Remember Embrace

Dream Journal: A Guided Journal for Recording and Reflecting on Your Dreams
Unlock the mysteries of your subconscious with this beautifully designed dream journal!

Dream Journal: Dream Relax Reflect Remember Embrace

Dream Journal: A Guided Journal for Recording and Reflecting on Your Dreams
Unlock the mysteries of your subconscious with this beautifully designed dream journal!

The Lost Keys To Thinking Like A Problem-Solver: How To Approach Problems, Break Them Down, And Find Solutions
The Lost Keys To Thinking Like A Problem-Solver: How To Approach Problems

Problem-solving isn't just about finding answers—it's about learning how to think.
Ever lost your keys, retraced your steps, and somehow still couldn't find them—only to realize they were right in front of you the whole time? Or spent hours stuck on a frustrating problem

at work, only to discover you were looking in the wrong place all along?

Printed in Dunstable, United Kingdom